IMACES *of*

HISTORIC SYDNEY

RANNIE GILLIS

NIMBUS
PUBLISHING

Nimbus Publishing Limited
PO Box 9166
Halifax, NS   B3K 5M8
(902) 455-4286

Printed and bound in Canada
Design: Peggy Issenman

Cover photo: Moxham's Castle, which overlooked Sydney Harbour, was destroyed by fire in 1966.

Title page photo: This Department of National Defence aerial photo from the 1930s was taken from a point over Hardwood Hill, looking north. George Street cuts a swath through the heart of the city. In less than ten years the south arm of the harbour would be filled with large numbers of ships waiting to join convoys heading overseas to fight in World War Two.

National Library of Canada Cataloguing in Publication Data

Gillis, Rannie
Historic Sydney / Rannie Gillis.
(Images of our past)
ISBN 1-55109-459-2

1. Sydney (N.S.)—History. I. Title. II. Series.
FC2349.S93G44 2003   971.6'95   C2003-905025-4

We acknowledge the financial support of the Government of Canada through the Book Publishing Industry Development Program (BPIDP) and the Canada Council for our publishing activities.

This book is dedicated to Ann Marie MacLean and Maria

Acknowledgements

This book would not have been possible without the help and encouragement of the following individuals. They gave freely of their time and expertise in providing photographs, archival research material, computers and scanners, and their own valuable insights and knowledge into the history of Sydney and surrounding area.

The staff of the Beaton Institute at the University College of Cape Breton: Sheldon MacInnes, acting director, Anne MacLean, Anne Connell, Lori Fitzgerald, Geoff Martin; the staff of the Old Sydney Society: Peyton Chisholm, curator, Dr. Robert Morgan, Elaine Hummer, Mary Gillis, and Pam Newton; Ian MacIntosh and Don Wood from the McConnell Library (Sydney); Dorothy and Howie Hoban for information and photos with regard to the Kelly Studio (Sydney); John Morrison, Allan Morrison, and Mike Sullivan from Quality Cameras (Sydney); Warren Gordon and Murdock Smith from Gordon Photographic (Sydney); Neil Libbey, for his knowledge and photos of early Sydney, especially with regard to the history of the Royal Cape Breton Yacht Club; Kristy Read, a graphic arts graduate who, with proficiency and skill, scanned 144 images—in only two days!

Finally, a very special thank you to the members of my family, especially my mother, Mary (MacLean) Gillis, my sister, Catherine Gillis, and my brother, Malcolm Gillis. Their interest and encouragement kept me going during those long winter days and nights.

Contents

Population: CBRM and Sydney

The CBRM (Cape Breton Regional Municipality) includes the city of Sydney, North Sydney, Sydney Mines, New Waterford, Dominion, Glace Bay, Louisbourg, and the rest of Cape Breton County. The CBRM came into existence on August 1, 1995, through the amalgamation of these eight municipalities. The CBRM is the second largest municipality in Nova Scotia, with an area of 2,470 square kilometres.

These statistics are from the National Census, held every ten years in Canada beginning in 1871. The figures for 1891 represent the population of Sydney before the construction of the steel plant.

Year	Sydney	CBRM
1891	2,427	34,244
1911	17,723	73,330
1941	28,305	110,703
1961	33,617	131,507
2001	23,990	109,330

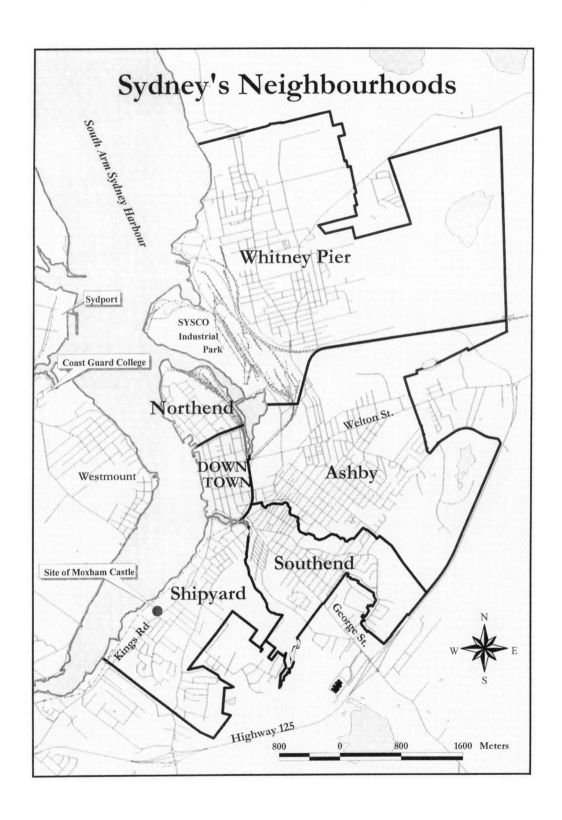

Sydney's Neighbourhoods

South Arm Sydney Harbour

Whitney Pier

Sydport

SYSCO Industrial Park

Coast Guard College

Northend

Welton St.

Westmount

DOWN TOWN

Ashby

Site of Moxham Castle

Southend

Shipyard

George St.

Kings Rd

Highway 125

800   0   800   1600 Meters

N
W   E
S

Introduction

M ost Canadians would not immediately think of Sydney, Nova Scotia, if asked to make a list of the most important military cities in the nation. In fact, on several occasions Sydney has displaced Halifax as the most essential seaport on Canada's east coast. There are good reasons for this. Not only is Sydney closer to Europe than any other port on the mainland of North America, but its strategic location at the entrance to the Gulf of St. Lawrence means that it also controls access to the St. Lawrence River and the industrial heartland of central Canada. Also, Sydney and its surrounding areas were the industrial centre of eastern Canada during both world wars of the twentieth century. The Sydney steel plant produced one-third of all the nation's steel, and the many mines of the Sydney Coal Fields produced tremendous amounts of coal, a mineral resource that was vital to the nation's war effort.

Equally important, from a military point of view, the south and west arms of Sydney Harbour could easily accommodate more than 100 cargo ships, a critical factor when it came to the formation of Trans-Atlantic convoys. The use of convoys to escort merchant ships across the Atlantic Ocean did not come into effect until three years after the outbreak of World War One. This new European conflict required large amounts of military and civilian supplies, most of which came from Canada and the United States. By 1917 German submarines were sinking so many supply ships that a convoy system was put in place in order to protect Allied shipping.

The main convoy assembly points in Canada were Sydney and Halifax, and the defences of these two harbours were quickly upgraded to provide secure gathering places for civilian ships preparing to cross the Atlantic Ocean. Sydney's strategic position on the eastern shore of the continent meant that it was the preferred port for Canadian and American ships to gather, except when ice conditions in the winter months closed the harbour and the Gulf of St. Lawrence. (St. John's, Newfoundland, was for the most part an assembly and refuelling point for naval escort vessels.)

During World War Two the convoy system was split into two distinct components. The fast convoys, containing ships which could maintain a speed of at least ten knots, sailed from Halifax. The slow convoys, with ships that travelled at a reduced rate of speed, left from Sydney.

Although Sydney's wartime efforts have often been eclipsed by those of its mainland sister, Halifax, for most of the last two hundred years Sydney Harbour played an important role in the defence policy of the British Empire, and, later, Canada. This role was often not fully acknowledged during peacetime; it is no wonder, then, that a prominent Canadian historian referred to Sydney Harbour during the nineteenth century as an "orphan outpost."

Sydney Harbour is actually the fifth name that has been attached to this body of water. To the early Mi'kmaq it was "Cibou," meaning river or inlet. On Nicholas Deny's map of 1672 it is called "La Rivière Denys." During the seventeenth century, when it was often visited by seasonal fishermen from Spain, it was known as "Spanish Bay." In a later description of Cape Breton Island, it is referred to as "Dartmouth Harbour."

In the two-hundred-year period after John Cabot's arrival in 1497, Cape Breton was frequently visited by European fishermen. They came over each spring, fished for the season, and returned home each fall with their small ships loaded down with the catch from the Grand Banks of Newfoundland and various inshore fisheries. As far as we know they never established any permanent winter fishing stations. They stayed in Newfoundland or stopped at Cape Breton to salt and dry their fish before the long voyage home.

In order to forestall the possibility of any friction developing between these fishermen, a "gentleman's agreement" was reached between them regarding the use of the harbours. Louisbourg was given to the English, while the French received St. Anne's Bay. The largest and safest bay was given to Spain, and for the next several centuries Sydney Harbour was known as Spanish Bay, or Spanish River (Sydney River). In spite of the fact that their respective nations were often at war, this plan worked very well, and each nation went about its own business (at least with regard to the fisheries).

All that would change in 1713 when the Treaty of Utrecht gave France complete control of Cape Breton Island, St. Pierre and Miquelon, and fishing rights to the west and northeast coasts of Newfoundland. The French government then decided that Louisbourg would become the capital of their new colony, and in 1720 they began to build a fortress on the shore of Louisbourg Harbour. Construction would continue for more than twenty years, but upon completion Louisbourg became the largest and most heavily fortified town in the New World.

By the mid-1730s the British government had become suspicious of French military power in North America, as well as its dominant position in the local fishery. And, by the early 1740s, business interests in the New England colonies were increasing the pressure on England to take action with regard to "the French Problem."

In 1744, England and France declared war on each other, and less than one year later a combined British and American force captured Fortress Louisbourg after a prolonged siege. However, much to the disgust of their American counterparts, the entire fortified town was returned to France, undamaged and intact, after a peace treaty was signed in 1748.

In 1749 the British government decided to fortify the fine natural harbour at Halifax, and set up a base for the Royal Navy. The construction of this facility would serve two purposes: it would protect the New England Colonies from the possible threat of an attack from Louisbourg, and it would provide a supply base for the British fishing fleets operating in the New World.

War between the two nations broke out again in 1756, and two years later, after the French garrison was defeated in the second siege of Louisbourg, the fortress was blown up by British Army engineers. With the end of the Seven Years' War, in 1763, France gave up all claims in North America, but was permitted to keep St. Pierre and Miquelon as fishing stations. Cape Breton, along with the rest of North America, became British.

Things were not going well, however, for the Thirteen (British) Colonies located almost a thousand miles to the south. There was widespread dissatisfaction with the mother country, and social, economic, and political changes were in the wind. Finally, in 1775, the American colonies declared war against Great Britain, and one year later came the famous "Declaration of Independence."

This revolutionary war lasted eight years. When the British finally capitulated, in 1883, many thousand loyal British subjects left the new United States and made their way into eastern Canada. Many of these Loyalists came to mainland Nova Scotia and Cape Breton Island.

This possibility was anticipated by the British government. With this in mind, Lord Sydney, the new secretary of state for the colonies, decided to grant provincial status to Cape Breton in the spring of 1784. It became official one year later, and for the next thirty-five years (1785–1820) Cape Breton Island was a separate colony under the British Crown.

Lord Sydney also appointed Major Joseph Frederick DesBarres as governor of the new province, and in 1785 the new governor chose the little peninsula in the south arm of Spanish Bay as his capital. A master mariner who had spent more than twenty years surveying the coast of Nova Scotia for the Royal Navy, DesBarres knew the area intimately. He decided to name the harbour and the new settlement "Sydney," after the new colonial secretary.

DesBarres lived to be 103 (1721–1824), and was to play an important part in the history of Cape Breton and Nova Scotia during his long life. Although born in Switzerland, he attended the Royal Military Academy in England, and after graduation started his career as a naval officer and military engineer. He was with General Wolfe at the second siege of Louisbourg and later took part in the successful capture of Quebec.

Fortunately for Sydney, DesBarres was also a trained surveyor, and based his plan for the new settlement on the British city of Bath. As a result, Sydney featured a proper grid design, with broad avenues and streets that intersected at right angles. Also included were plenty of open or "common" spaces.

There were several reasons why DesBarres chose Sydney over Louisbourg as the location of his new capital. First and foremost was the large harbour, the innermost reaches of which offered superb protection from severe storms. Second, unlike Louisbourg with its stunted growth, the harbour at Sydney was surrounded by thick forest, with many large trees, which could provide an excellent source of timber for the construction of ships. Third, the soil in the vicinity was quite fertile, unlike

This scene is reproduced from an original painting in the Webster Collection in the New Brunswick Museum, Saint John, NB, which was made by Lieut. Booth, a British officer, in August 1785. It shows the clearing being made on the wooded banks and the first buildings erected; the largest, on the right, being the residence of Governor DesBarres. The tents of the 33rd Regiment are seen. The two vessels at anchor have brought Lieut.-Gen. Campbell, Commander-in-Chief from Halifax, on a visit of inspection.

the barren, rocky, outcrops at Louisbourg. The new settlement would therefore be able to grow most of the food required for its own upkeep.

Approximately 140 Loyalists arrived with DesBarres, including a small number who brought their own slaves. Each, including the slaves, were given three years' worth of clothing and supplies by the British government. A group of soldiers from the British garrison in Halifax also arrived, and promptly began the construction of simple wooden barracks and a mess hall.

Their first winter on the island was not an easy one. Many of the new crops failed, and at one point Governor DesBarres was forced to send an armed party overland to Arichat, where a Quebec-owned ship was stuck in the ice. Faced with the option of having his cargo of food expropriated by the British Crown, the captain offered to sell his entire ship and cargo (minus crew) instead. When the offer was accepted, the vessel was cut out of the ice and sailed around to Louisbourg. Because Sydney Harbour was blocked with ice, the food supplies were then hauled overland to Sydney on wooden sledges.

By 1790 the population of Sydney was 121 individuals, of whom 26 were preparing to leave! The little village also had a total of 81 houses, one-third of which were listed as "uninhabitable."

Then, in 1802, a vessel from Scotland landed 299 immigrants, in a resumption of direct emigration from that country. More Scottish settlers arrived and by 1833 there were about sixty inhabitable homes in the town, as well as an army barracks (Victoria Park), courthouse, several stores, and three churches. In 1854, as a result of the Crimean War, the last soldiers of the Sydney Garrison were called away and the original Victoria Park Barracks were closed.

Many in Sydney thought that the loss of the military would mean the end of their little town. And nothing much happened for the next half century to change this rather bleak outlook. Sydney remained a small village, far removed from the centre of political, military, and economic life in Halifax. Fortunately, coal mining would soon provide an economic boom.

Although there are no coal deposits in Sydney itself, the extensive reserves in the surrounding towns and villages of North Sydney, Sydney Mines, Florence, New Waterford, and Glace Bay are collectively known as the Sydney Coal Fields.

For more than two centuries, from approximately 1750 to 1950, this area was the largest coal-producing region in Canada, with more than seventy mines in operation over that period. The highest yearly output in the Sydney Coal Fields was in 1913, when an astonishing 5.75 million tonnes were mined. Even as late as 1960 it still provided one-third of the annual coal production in the country.

Over the years it is estimated that more than three hundred million tonnes of coal have been removed from the Sydney Coal Fields. Even so, the Government of Canada has estimated that more than one billion tonnes of coal remain, enough to produce several million tonnes per year for the next two hundred years!

This coal is of the bituminous or "soft" variety, and is the most important and most plentiful type of coal in North America. It contains a greater amount of combustible material, and a smaller amount of ash, than anthracite or "hard" coal. However, it usually contains more sulfur, which makes it unsuitable for certain applications.

With the rapid expansion of the island's coal mining industry in the mid-1800s, the mines around Sydney Harbour attracted the excess population from the overpopulated rural areas.

With the advent of railways in the latter part of the nineteenth century, Sydney became a very important port, especially for the shipping of coal. The Sydney and Louisbourg railroad was opened in 1877, and by 1891 there was regular train service between Sydney and Halifax. The establishment of a steel plant in 1902 marked the beginning of a period of real economic prosperity, which resulted in a rapid increase in population.

In order to make steel, three raw materials are required: coal, iron ore, and limestone. Coal was in abundance, and large quantities of limestone were available at Marble Mountain on the Bras d'Or Lakes and George's River on the Northside. Although there are no iron ore deposits in Cape

Breton, large quantities of a very high quality iron ore were available at Bell Island in Newfoundland. It could be shipped to Sydney Harbour at a very reasonable cost.

As in the case of wartime convoys, Sydney Harbour's excellent location on Canada's eastern seaboard was a major consideration in the location of the most modern and technologically advanced iron and steel mill in North America. Not only was the harbour one of the best and safest on the Atlantic seaboard, but the vast reserves of the Sydney Coal Fields were the only ones in North America that were located directly on the ocean.

Construction of this world-class facility started in 1899 and was finished three years later. Built by the Dominion Iron and Steel Company, this industrial project covered about five hundred acres, and extended for almost two miles along the east side of Sydney Harbour and Muggah Creek. For a fee of $85,000 the town of Sydney expropriated the land from the individuals who owned it, and donated it without charge to the company. The town council also voted to exempt the company from paying taxes on property, income, and earnings for a period of at least thirty years. In the press of the day Sydney was referred to as, "the Pittsburgh of the North!"

With the construction of the steel plant, and the emergence of related industries, the new city experienced rapid growth in population, especially in the Whitney Pier area. Thousands of skilled and unskilled workers flocked to Sydney to fill the new jobs that were available. Many of these jobs were filled by Gaelic-speaking Scots or French-speaking Acadians from the surrounding rural areas in Cape Breton, while others went to able-bodied individuals from the nearby colony of Newfoundland. Most jobs, however, went to immigrants from outside North America, and it was largely this group that gave such an international flavour to life in "The Pier."

They came from all over: Italy, Ukraine, Ireland, Poland, Croatia, Lebanon, Slovakia, Bulgaria, Czechoslovakia, Serbia, Slovenia, Greece, and Russia. Blacks, mostly from Barbados in the West Indies, also moved to the Pier. A significant number of Jewish people came from the Middle East and Central Europe. The resultant population growth in Sydney was nothing short of amazing. In 1899, before the construction of the steel plant, Sydney was a small, relatively unimportant town of around 2,500 people. Ten years later (1909) it was a vibrant, cosmopolitan city of more than 16,000 individuals.

By 1912, the Sydney steel plant was making nearly half of all the steel in Canada. At its peak, the plant could make 800,000 tonnes of pig iron and 900,000 tonnes of crude steel yearly. By the end of the First World War (1918) Sydney had a population of about 20,000. However, with the end of hostilities the local economy entered a period of shrinkage and decline, and big changes were on the horizon. In 1920 the island's two major employers, the Nova Scotia Steel and Coal Company and the Dominion

AERIAL PHOTO OF SYDNEY, 1930S

This panoramic aerial shot from the 1930s gives a view of the Sydney waterfront, from Wentworth Park in the lower right to the North End on the left. The curve where King's Road ends and the Esplanade begins. It also gives a bird's-eye view of the Sydney Steel Plant, the largest single-industry industrial facility in eastern Canada. Construction started in 1899 and the first steel was made in 1901. By 1912 Sydney Steel was producing almost half of all the steel made in Canada! The plant was in operation for exactly one hundred years, until its closure in 2001. The Muggah Creek watershed, between the steel plant and the North End, is plainly visible in the centre of the picture. Today this same watershed is known as the infamous Sydney Tar Ponds, and has the dubious reputation of being the most toxic waste site in Canada.

Iron and Coal Company, were taken over and incorporated into a huge new industrial conglomerate known as the British Empire Steel Company.

Although the city's population declined somewhat, especially during the Great Depression in the 1930s, the outbreak of the Second World War in 1939 led to a resurgence in activity at the steel plant and in the local coal mines. By 1950 the population of Sydney was approximately 35,000, with more than 4,000 men employed at Sydney Steel.

There were ominous warning signs on the horizon, however. In 1950, coal supplied fifty-two per cent of Canada's energy demands. By 1957 the arrival of cheap imported oil had reduced that figure to just twenty-five per cent. In the 1950s the national railroads began the switch from coal-burning steam engines to the newer, oil-burning diesel locomotives. The local coal mines were in deep trouble, and unemployment was on the rise.

Events took another turn for the worse in 1967 when the British owners of Sydney's obsolete steel plant walked away from the aging business. As a result of massive public protests, and fear of social and political unrest in the industrial heart of Cape Breton Island, the Nova Scotia Government reluctantly agreed to take over the once cutting-edge but now antiquated and old-fashioned steel plant.

A new firm was created, the Sydney Steel Corporation (SYSCO). In spite of huge financial losses, the provincial government continued to run the steel plant until they finally threw in the towel in 2001. Unable to find a buyer for the dilapidated complex, the government sold off the equipment. The plant is in the process of being dismantled. A century of steel making in Sydney has come to an end!

Today, with a population of approximately 25,000, Sydney remains the economic and social centre of southeastern Cape Breton. As such it provides a wide range of facilities for both residents and visitors, including a recently enlarged public wharf to accommodate the increasing number of cruise ships that visit the city each year.

Indeed, the tourism and cultural sector, best exemplified by the annual success of the Celtic Colours Festival, is one of several areas that will continue to play an expanding role in Sydney's economic future. This, along with the possibility of future economic benefits from the expected development of the offshore oil and gas industry, should only bode well for the destiny of this historic seaport.

Chapter 1

Sydney Business District

CHARLOTTE STREET, 1930

Several "Model-T" vintage automobiles line the east side of Charlotte Street in this 1930 scene. On the far left is the domed roof of the Bank of Montreal. The large four-story building is the Pistone Block, with the three-story wooden Burchell Block to its right. Turnbull's Drug Store is in the stone building on the right.

SONS OF TEMPERANCE SLEIGH RIDE, CHARLOTTE STREET, C.1883

In this charming photograph, bundled-up members of the Sons of Temperance cross the old Charlotte Street bridge, back at a time when horse and sleigh was the primary means of local winter travel. Organized in 1849, the Sydney division of the Sons of Temperance did not at first demand total abstinence. Rather, they simply pledged to drink no more than four glasses of rum each day! Thirty years later, when total abstinence came into effect, they would often draw more than two thousand individuals to their annual parade.

This intriguing photograph appears to have been taken from an upstairs window in the old courthouse, located just inside the entrance to Victoria Park in the city's north end. The picture is especially interesting because of the presence of the old three-masted sailing ship and the new steam-powered, ocean-going freighter. While the sailing ship required nothing but a good wind, the steamer required coal, and lots of it.

While the older vessels would often stop in Sydney to pick up fresh water and other supplies, the newer steam ships usually stopped in only to pick up "bunker coal," which they could easily obtain from the International Coal and Railway Company pier in the upper left-hand corner of the scene.

CHARLOTTE STREET, 1890

This fascinating photograph, with such a wealth of information and period detail, was taken near the lower end of Charlotte Street. The very unusual steam engine marks the present location of the Vogue Theater, while the YMCA is located on the right side, just out of the picture. The three-story building on the left corner, behind the "window glass" building, is the present location of the law firm Khattar & Khattar.

The engine is a unique double-ended and double-boilered "Fairlie" locomotive brought to Sydney from England by the coal company.

The photo, looking north up Charlotte Street, shows the old bridge over the rail line that ran to the shipping piers of the International Coal and Railway Company at the foot of Falmouth Street. At top right, the cupola on the roof of Holy Angels Convent is visible.

The picture was taken by a local photographer named Umlah, whose studio was located in the building with "Window Glass" written on the side. There is a roofless building just behind the train.

INNES STORE,
C.1900

The Innes Store at the corner of Pitt and Charlotte Street was part of the Miles Block.

SYDNEY'S GREAT FIRE, 1901

A view of the still smoldering ruins on Charlotte Street, looking north from Wentworth Street.

On the morning of October 19, 1901, a pot of melted glue resulted in a raging fire that destroyed a total of seventy-eight wooden buildings in downtown Sydney. The glue was being heated on an oil stove in the back of a furniture store when it was accidentally tipped over. The building was quickly engulfed by flames and, as the fire quickly spread from one structure to another, a mini "fire-storm" developed that completely wiped out several business blocks. There was almost total destruction in the area enclosed by Charlotte, Pitt, Wentworth, and Bentinck streets. In spite of the great amount of damage, no lives were lost, and only a few private homes went up in flames. The affected area was quickly rebuilt with modern brick buildings, thanks to the affluence brought by the new steel industry.

**BANK OF
MONTREAL,
1901**

The classically inspired Bank of Montreal, on the corner of Charlotte and
Dorchester streets, was built in 1899. One of the most architecturally
significant buildings in the downtown core, its construction was proof
of the banking industry's belief in the new role of Sydney as the iron and
steel centre of eastern Canada. The exterior of the building is of carved
sandstone, while the domed roof was covered in copper sheeting. Inside,
the vaulted ceiling creates a profound sense of space and openness. Other
classic architectural details include the palladium windows, ionic columns,
and the triangular, gable-like pediments which form the roof line on the
four sides of the building. Still in use, the building reflects the unique
historical legacy of this prime commercial location while offering the most
up-to-date banking facilities.

PROWSE BROTHERS & CROWELLS, 1902

The workmen involved in the construction of this impressive building pose for a group photo in the spring of 1902. This was the second department store built by the Prowse and Crowell families, on the same location on Charlotte Street. The first, smaller store burnt down in the great fire of 1901. A temporary store is partly visible to the right of this photograph. The enterprise continued, under the Crowells name, until the closing years of the twentieth century. At the present time (2003) the property is for sale, at a price of approximately $350,000.

PROWSE BROTHERS & CROWELLS, INTERIOR

The new Prowse Brothers & Crowells store covered three floors, and almost a thousand different items were in stock. Clothing and housewares, construction tools and farm implements, the finest china and the latest books—all this and much more was available to the citizens of Sydney and surrounding areas. The "Moosehead" sign and logo in the centre of the picture is an advertisement for the "Moosehead Fur Company" of Montreal, not for the alcoholic beverage of the same name!

PROWSE BROTHERS & CROWELLS

The twenty-one staff members of Prowse Brothers & Crowells gather in front of their new store on Charlotte Street.

CHARLOTTE STREET LOOKING NORTH, C.1903

In this photo, taken at the junction of Charlotte and Pitt streets, one of the new electric streetcars is seen approaching in the distance. It is interesting to speculate on the effect that this new form of silent transportation had on the horses parked along the side of the street. The three-story brick building on the left is the Commercial Bank, while the Sydney Court House can be seen in the distance.

CHARLOTTE
STREET
LOOKING
SOUTH, C.1903
A city of domes? Not really, but in this turn-of-the-twentieth-century photograph taken from a window in the old courthouse, three domed buildings are visible. The Royal Bank on the right, the post office on the left, and the Bank of Montreal in the centre.

Where is the traffic? An electric streetcar is seen approaching the intersection of Charlotte and Dorchester streets, while two horses are seen in the foreground. One wonders what the original photographer would make of the same scene, exactly one hundred years later, and the very high volume of automobile traffic on a summer Saturday night?

Charlotte and Dorchester
Sts. Sydney, N. S.

**ELECTRIC
STREETCAR,
CHARLOTTE AND
DORCHESTER,
1914**

A very interesting picture because of the fascinating juxtaposition of three land-based forms of transportation used in downtown Sydney: on the far right a gasoline-powered automobile, or motor-car as they were often called back then; to its immediate left a horse-powered wagon, which by this date was rapidly becoming restricted to the rural areas surrounding Sydney; and, dominating the centre of the scene, an electric streetcar (tramcar), which used electricity to provide a relatively quiet form of transit around the city.

The buildings in this photograph all played an important part in the business and legal life of the young industrial city: on the left the Canadian Bank of Commerce (as it was originally known); just behind it the Royal Bank, with its distinctive domed cupola; and on the right, the courthouse, which burned down in 1959.

CHARLOTTE STREET SNOWSTORM, 1918

In this typical winter scene, looking north from the corner of Charlotte and Wentworth streets, workmen clear the tracks for the electric streetcars. In the days before mechanized snow removal, the streets of Sydney would often remain covered in deep snow for several days after each snowstorm. The present-day YMCA is located on the extreme right, just out of the picture.

MORLEY'S GROCERY STORE, 1920

A charming interior view of Morley's Grocery Store on Charlotte Street, only two years after the end of the First World War. The owner, Fred Morley, is standing with his hands on his hips, to the right of the stack of Kellogg's Toasted Corn Flakes. Directly in front of him, on the floor, is the pickle barrel, while a batch of fresh bananas hangs from the ceiling, next to a stack of Jell-O boxes.

CHARLOTTE
STREET
LOOKING
SOUTH, C.1930

The busy intersection of Charlotte and Dorchester streets, on a cold winter day in 1930. A vintage bus and several automobiles maneuver along the congested street, long before the advent of traffic lights. The overhead wires provide power to the electric streetcars, which still ran on tracks up the centre of the street. The Bank of Montreal, with its domed roof, is on the left.

ANDERSON'S
POINT, C.1890

Two schooners under full sail grace this scene of Anderson's Point in the North End. The view is north, across the south arm of the harbour towards Point Edward. This would later be the location of the Sydney Engineering and Drydock facility.

ANDERSON'S
POINT, C.1927

This photo shows the north end of the Esplanade before the erection of the Sydney Engineering and Drydock, just to the north of the present-day Government Wharf.

TANNERY BRIDGE, KING'S ROAD, 1889

A solitary horse and wagon ramble over the Tannery Bridge at Wentworth Park, where King's Road meets the Esplanade. The bridge was named after the tannery, the large structure on the left. In the top left is the wooden shipping pier built by the International Coal and Railway Company in 1870. The railroad leading to the pier ran through the property presently occupied by the YMCA on Charlotte Street.

In the years immediately after the founding of Sydney, when the area around the creek was thickly forested, this region provided most of the timber needed for the construction of new homes and businesses. These first-growth trees, much larger than any seen today, also led to the development of a substantial shipbuilding industry in the area, to the west of the creek. The shipyard was along the shore, and the area in back, where the shipyard workers built their own homes, is still referred to today as the shipyard.

The first ship constructed in the shipyard was the brig *Nancy*, of one hundred tonnes, built in 1790 by Philip Ingoville. Over the next one hundred years, approximately eighty-six ships were built in the shipyard.

SYDNEY COAL YARD, BYNG AVENUE, C.1900

In this pleasant winter scene, hopper cars from the Intercolonial Railway prepare to deliver their cargo of coal to waiting teams of horses and wagons, which would then deliver their valuable loads to homes and businesses in Sydney and vicinity. Coal was the primary means of heating structures in Sydney at that time, although rural homes usually used firewood.

INTERNATIONAL SHIPPING PIER, C.1900

This substantial wooden pier, located at the foot of Falmouth Street, was built in 1870. Moored alongside it is a large, ocean-going steamship, taking on board a large amount of coal for its steam engine, before heading out across the Atlantic Ocean to the British Isles. The little wharf, centre right, was known as the LeCras Wharf.

SYDNEY HOTEL, 1902   Built in 1896, at a cost of $40,000, this rather ornate wooden structure was considered to be one of the few first-class hotels in the Maritime Provinces. Designed in the Queen Anne style prevalent at the time, it was noted for its spacious wrap-around verandah and its four stylish towers. It was one of the first hotels in Eastern Canada to have electric lights, as well as hot and cold running water in all the guest rooms. In its first full year of operation, more than six thousand guests stayed at the elegant facility, with daily room rates starting at $2.00! The hotel was destroyed by fire in 1918.

ORANGEMEN'S
PARADE,
ESPLANADE,
C.1904

The first Orange Lodge was organized in Northern Ireland in 1795, to commemorate the earlier defeat of Catholic forces at the hands of Protestant troops under King William of Orange. Local lodges soon sprang up all over Ireland, and followed Irish immigrants to the New World. Fortunately, the annual Orangemen's parade that was held in Sydney was a peaceful affair, and did not involve any intimidation or threat of violence, as was common in the old country.

The sign on the barn, behind the six horse-and-wagon combinations, reads: "Hillman's Truck (freight wagon), Hack (taxi), and Livery Stables." The horse and wagon remained the basic means of transportation in Sydney from the time of its founding to the early years of the twentieth century. Even after the advent of the railroad and the electric streetcar, the horse and wagon continued to be the primary means of travel between Sydney and its surrounding rural areas.

SYDNEY FIRE
BRIGADE, 1909

The first big fire in Sydney was in 1851, when four buildings on the Esplanade burned to the ground. There was no fire fighting apparatus, but the Black Watch Highlanders from Victoria Park came quickly to the rescue with a military fire engine. If they hadn't, the damage would have been considerably greater. One year later the military donated their equipment to the town, and a proper fire brigade was organized at the corner of Amelia and Charlotte streets. After the great fire in 1901, a new fire station was built on Bentinck Street. It remained in use until 1982. In this photograph, members of the fire brigade are decked out in their formal attire in preparation for a Dominion Day parade.

SILVER THAW   This charming winter scene, with everything covered by a "silver thaw," was taken in the early years of the twentieth century. It shows the Esplanade looking north from Dorchester Street. The Sydney Marine Terminal, where the cruise ships now dock, is located just to the left of this picture.

ROBERTSON BLOCK, 1917   The horse and wagon used to deliver groceries for A.W. Meikle waits in front of Meikle's store at the corner of George and Prince streets in Sydney. Using motorized vehicles for delivery purposes did not become a reality until the late 1920s, and then only for larger stores or wholesale operations.

GOVERNMENT WHARF, 1939

Construction work on the new Government Wharf on the eve of the oubreak of World War Two. The presence of a "Great Lakes" boat in the background, tied up to Harrington's Wharf, makes this an unusual photograph. Such long and narrow boats, built to navigate the restricted locks on the Great Lakes shipping lanes, are not really suitable for ocean transit or operation in the Gulf of St. Lawrence. Only on very rare occasions does a "Laker" visit the east coast of Canada. When completed, the wharf would quickly be taken over by the Canadian military, as Sydney Harbour prepared for its role as a major convoy port between Canada and the British Isles.

SYDNEY, N.S.

SYDNEY COURT HOUSE, 1938

This rooftop photo, taken from an unusual angle, gives an excellent view of the old Sydney Court House (1913), which was destroyed by fire in November 1959. At that time the building also housed the Sydney Library in its basement, and more than 80,000 books were lost. These printed volumes, many of them quite old, were to be transferred to the new library which was then under construction. The new library was funded by a gift from former Sydney mayor James McConnell.

This image also brings back special memories for the author. In September 1959, he had just started studies as a first-year student at Xavier Junior College, and was researching his first major term paper in the basement of the courthouse. He lost six weeks' worth of research in the fire when he left his work in the library overnight.

Xavier Junior College was located in the former Lyceum Theater on George Street, the top corner of which is just visible in the centre right of this picture. Also prominent are the twin spires of Sacred Heart Catholic Church, and the belching smokestacks of the blast furnace at the Sydney Steel Plant in Whitney Pier.

Chapter 2

Sydney Steel

SYDNEY STEEL, C.1902, THE PITTSBURGH OF THE NORTH

The brand new, state-of-the-art iron and steel plant was built in Sydney by the Dominion Iron and Steel Company. The large smoke stacks (two hundred feet tall) indicate the location of the four blast furnaces. To the right of these is the power house, and on the far right is the open hearth.

This industrial project, which at the time was the largest and most modern in Canada, covered about five hundred acres, and extended for almost two miles along the shoreline of Sydney Harbour and Muggah Creek. The company was formed by a special act passed by the Canadian parliament, with an initial capitalization of $25 million. The Nova Scotia Legislature also agreed to reduce the proposed "royalty fee per ton" paid to the provincial government by fifty per cent for a period of eight years.

Construction of this world-class facility started in 1899 and was finished three years later. For a fee of $85,000, the town of Sydney expropriated the land from the individuals who owned it, and donated it without charge to the company. The town council also voted to exempt the company from paying taxes on property, income, and earnings for a period of at least thirty years.

In addition to the four blast furnaces and ten open hearth furnaces, the plant consists of four hundred coke ovens; blooming, billets, wire, rod, and structural mills; foundry and machine shops; two iron ore piers; twenty-five miles of railroad tracks; and a large general office building.

SYDNEY STEEL,
1899 AND 1901

These two photographs show a panoramic view of the shoreline of Muggah Creek, on the east side of the harbour, before and after the construction of the Sydney Steel complex. The upper photo shows a quiet country scene, with coal-shipping piers visible on the left. In the lower image are the four stacks of the blast furnaces, as well as the open hearth, coke ovens, and machine shops.

CONSTRUCTION OF SHIPPING PIERS, 1900

A great "industrial" photograph showing the massive iron girders that were used in the construction of the lower levels of the shipping piers for the new steel plant at Whitney Pier. These iron girders came from a mill in New York, and arrived in Sydney Harbour by ship.

SHIPPING PIERS AT WHITNEY PIER

The two piers at right were built by the Dominion Coal Company. Coal from the company's six mines in the Glace Bay and New Waterford areas was shipped from these piers to destinations in Canada and the United States. These wooden piers, built of southern pine on solid foundations that extended into the bedrock beneath the harbour, could handle up to six steam ships at one time. The two piers at left, the most modern in North America, were built to service the facilities of the Dominion Iron and Steel Company, between 1899 and 1901. The pier in the left centre handled the iron ore that arrived by boat from Bell Island, Newfoundland. The pier on the far left was used for the shipment of iron and steel products to markets all over the world.

SYDNEY COKE OVENS, 1900

A slab of coke, just after it was "pushed" out of a coke oven. Coal must be refined into coke before it can be used in a blast furnace. This is done by heating the coal in an oven for at least forty-eight hours, in order to remove any impurities. More than four hundred coke ovens were in use at the Sydney steel plant when this section of the mill opened in 1900.

When it comes out of the ground, iron ore is only about fifty per cent pure. A blast furnace takes that iron ore, heats it with coke and limestone, and converts it into iron that is about ninety-five per cent pure. This "pig iron" is used for iron girders, iron rails, etc. The pig iron could also be sent along to the open hearth, to be made into steel.

Each blast furnace, in addition to the furnace itself, consisted of four hot-blast stoves. Each stove was a huge, steel, brick-lined device, standing more than one hundred feet tall. The "blast" or super hot air that would be blown into the furnace was first heated in the ovens. Each furnace required 4,000 pounds of iron ore, 2,300 pounds of coke, and 1,200 pounds of limestone in order to make one ton of iron. The temperature inside would reach 3,500 degrees Fahrenheit.

After the sod turning ceremony for the new steel plant was held on July 1, 1899, construction proceeded at a furious pace. This photograph was taken almost one year later, and shows the machine shop and power house of the new plant. It would take three years for the project to be completed.

LADLES AND
INGOT MOULDS

A view from the other end of the open hearth building, showing the huge fifty-ton ladles resting on the right, and on the left some of the moulds into which the molten steel was poured. When the steel cooled, the moulds would be removed, leaving a steel ingot. These ingots would then be shipped to other parts of the industrial complex for further refining into finished products.

OPEN HEARTH   This monstrous building, over eight hundred feet long, contained ten furnaces, each lined with fire-brick. Here pig iron from the blast furnace was re-heated with limestone, and scrap iron was added to the mix. After "cooking" for about ten hours, each furnace would tilt, or pivot, and pour the liquid steel into giant ladles. The ladles would then pour the molten steel into moulds to produce steel ingots.

POWER HOUSE   A view of the in-house electric power plant, housed in a separate building. The man standing next to the wall gives an indication of the size of the machinery used to produce power for the steel plant. In front of him can be seen the massive flywheels of the three large electric generators, each driven by its own steam-condensing engine.

More than fifty million gallons of water a day was required to operate the Dominion Iron and Steel Company operation in Sydney. Most of that was used to cool down the various mechanical aspects of the production process. However, several million gallons of that water were used, along with vast amounts of local coal, to produce steam to generate the large amounts of electricity required to operate the massive industrial complex.

AERIAL PHOTO, C.1932

An excellent low-level view of downtown Sydney, including the rail yards, the sprawling Sydney steel works, and parts of Whitney Pier on the horizon. George Street is the broad thoroughfare in the lower left, while at centre right the former Intercolonial Railroad Station, built in 1906, and the boxcars immediately behind it are visible. The magnitude of the steel plant is quite evident in this photo, as it stretches from the four tall smokestacks of the blast furnaces on the far left, to the large rectangular general office building on the far right. The area between the rail yards and the steel plant is the former Muggah Creek, which in seventy years would gain national notoriety as "Canada's worst toxic dump site." On the back of the photo in pencil is written "Sirka 1932."

Chapter 3

Transportation

MᴄLᴀᴜɢʜʟɪɴ, Bᴜɪᴄᴋ Rᴏᴀᴅsᴛᴇʀ (Tʜᴇ Gʀᴇʏ Gʜᴏsᴛ), ᴄ.1914

The McLaughlin Carriage Company of Oshawa, Ontario, was well known for the quality of their wagons and carriages. In 1907 they decided to produce a motor car—the first to be designed and built in Canada. With this in mind they signed a fifteen-year contract with the Buick Motor Company to provide engines and transmissions for the new vehicles. In their first year they built 154 McLaughlin-Buicks. The McLaughlin Carriage Company was sold to General Motors of Canada in 1918. This photo was taken on King's Road close to Moxham's Castle.

SS MARION, 1910

This interesting photograph of the "hustle-and-bustle" of a local pier was taken at Harrington's Wharf, on the lower Esplanade in Sydney. C.W. Harrington operated a wholesale business in flour and animal feed, and shipped goods from his wharf to all parts of Cape Breton Island. He became the first mayor of Sydney when the city was incorporated in 1885.

The S.S. *Marion* was a side-wheeler, purchased by the Bras d'Or Steamship Company in 1882. Built in New York State, the ship had originally served as an excursion boat on the Hudson River. After coming to Cape Breton, where it was refitted with staterooms and new furniture, it sailed between Sydney and Mulgrave, on the mainland.

By 1910 *Marion* was offering a tri-weekly service between Sydney Harbour and the Bras d'Or Lakes. Leaving Sydney early in the morning, it called at North Sydney, Big Bras d'Or, New Campbellton, Boulardarie Centre, Ross's Ferry, Big Harbour, Baddeck, Nyanza, and finally Whycocomagh, for the night. With a large saloon, dining room, and spacious staterooms, *Marion* was the finest of all the freight and passenger boats that ran on the Bras d'Or Lakes in the early years of the twentieth century. It was destroyed by fire on October 21, 1922, while at the wharf in Whycocomagh.

When the first settlers came to Cape Breton the land was covered by thick forest, right down to the water's edge. At first they used the water for local travel, travelling by canoe or their own little boats. By the mid-nineteenth century, however, regular scheduled public transportation was available on the island's waterways, especially the Bras d'Or Lakes. These services continued until the outbreak of the Second World War in 1939, by which time improved highways and the railroad made service by boat redundant.

THE *PAWNEE* ARRIVES, C.1915

An excellent photograph of the ferry *Pawnee* approaching the wharf of the Cape Breton Electric Company on the Esplanade. The *Pawnee,* which entered service in 1901, was the first ferry operated by the company. It offered an hourly service, beginning at 6:30 A.M., between Sydney and North Sydney, with frequent side trips to Whitney Pier and Point Edward. Judging by the flag on its stern, the large vessel behind it is a French battle cruiser, probably on a stopover to obtain bunker coal for its steam engines.

S.S. *PEERLESS*, C.1910

Built in 1886 specifically for the Cape Breton Electric Company, the steamship *Peerless* served on the Sydney-North Sydney run for forty-six years. On weekdays it made fourteen round-trips, on Sundays only five. It called also at Point Edward and Westmount, tides permitting. *Peerless* made its last crossing in 1932, after regular bus service was instituted between the two locations. In the background are the Sydney Hotel and the new Masonic Hall, with the circular dome on top.

In 1901 the Sydney Ferry Company was sold to the new Cape Breton
Electric Company. This firm operated an electric street trolley service
in Sydney, and another trolley service on the north side of the harbour,
between North Sydney and Sydney Mines. With the addition of the
ferry service, which operated several times a day between Sydney and
North Sydney, the company had a virtual monopoly with regard to
modern transportation methods in the industrial area. Ferry service was
also available to Whitney Pier, Westmount, and Point Edward. This
photograph, with visiting warships in the background, shows the corner
turret of the Royal Cape Breton Yacht Club on the right. Ferry service
continued on Sydney Harbour until 1947.

Aspy FERRY, C.1927

The *Aspy* was built in 1925 for the North Shore Steamship Company in Sydney, the second of three ships to bear the same name, all operating on a regular basis from Sydney to Ingonish, Neil's Harbour, Dingwall, and Bay St. Lawrence. The first *Aspy* sank in a vicious gale in 1924, off Cape North. This ship ran until the end of the Second World War, while the third *Aspy* ran from 1946 until the mid-1950s. By then improved highways had made the "down North ferries" redundant.

PACKARD AT MOXHAM'S CASTLE, 1909

This charming photo of a 1909 Packard "Touring Model" was taken outside the main gate at Moxham's Castle. In the early years of the twentieth century, the Packard was the most sought after "motor-car" among those striving for a symbol of status and success. The 1909 model was a superbly executed "classic" design, both aesthetically and otherwise. It sold for $4,200 (U.S.), at a time when the Ford Model "T" could be bought for $600! In addition to being the finest luxury car available in the United States, and perhaps the world, the 1909 Packard was also far ahead of the competition in terms of engineering innovations. It was the first to include headlamps as standard equipment, and the first to include a reserve fuel tank. The Packard was truly a "gentleman's car, built by gentlemen." (Notice that the steering wheel is on the right side of the car.)

It is somehow appropriate that the Packard automobile was first built in Ohio, the original home of Arthur Moxham. He had built a Scottish-style castle in Lorain, Ohio, and later had it dismantled and shipped to Sydney, where it was re-built at the present site of Cabot House on King's Road. As vice-president and general manager of the new steel plant, Arthur Moxham could certainly afford a new Packard!

Sydney's First Bus, 1912   This homemade bus, believed to be the first in Canada, made its maiden run on Labour Day, 1912. It picked up individuals on Charlotte Street (fee 5 cents), and dropped them off at the Cape Breton County Exhibition Grounds on King's Road (the former St. Rita Hospital site). The bus was built by J.A. McCallum, who owned a local carriage-building shop. It was equipped with solid rubber tires and ran on kerosene fuel. The driver in this photograph was Tom Mcgowan.

The Inter-Colonial Railway came about as a result of Confederation in 1867, when the new government of the Dominion of Canada decided to build a railway that would connect the Maritime Provinces with Central Canada and Quebec. Construction of this "Intercolonial" railway started immediately, but the tracks did not reach Sydney until 1891. With the rapid industrial growth of the city after 1900, the original brick station proved to be too small. By 1906 this impressive facility, built by the Chappell Brothers construction firm, had been completed. Its steeply pitched roof lines were examples of the Norman Gothic Chateau style, used in many railroad stations in Canada after the turn of the twentieth century.

Chapter 4

Sydney and the Military

36TH FIELD BATTERY, CADETS, 1915

While smartly dressed women and children watch, the officers and men of the 36th Field Battery are followed in their parade by a large troop of army cadets. While the First World War would be over before these young boys could be shipped overseas, they had no way of knowing that they would all come of age in time for the Second World War in 1939.

**VICTORIA PARK,
NORTH END
SYDNEY, 1889**

Officers and men of the Sydney Field Battery on parade in front of the old courthouse. Originally formed in 1883, on orders from the Canadian Department of Militia and Defence, the Sydney Field Battery had a complement of eighty officers and men. They were equipped with four bronze guns that fired a four-pound shot. In 1889 the inspector of artillery reported that "the Sydney Field Battery is still armed with obsolete guns, that were very inaccurate in their fire." He also said that the horses used to draw each gun were "under sized and too small." He did not realize that the battery had borrowed pit ponies from a local coal mine, as they did not have their own horses. In 1895 the Sydney Field Battery was renamed the 17th Field Battery (Sydney).

VICTORIA PARK, SENIOR NCOS, 1895

Often described as the most important men in any army, these three sergeants were senior NCOs (non-commissioned officers) with the 17th Field Battery (Sydney) stationed at Victoria Park. They were responsible for the day-to-day operation of the battery, and served as a liaison between the lower ranks and the officers. Left to right, they are S. Black, J. Pearson, and J. MacMullin.

17TH FIELD BATTERY (SYDNEY)

Non-commissioned officers (NCOs) and enlisted men of the 17th Field Battery pose at Victoria Park before shipping out for active duty in the Boer War in South Africa.

The small-scale conflict between new British settlers in South Africa and the descendants of the original Dutch settlers (Boers) lasted for three years (1899–1901). With the help of soldiers from Canada and several other British colonies, the Boer resistance collapsed, and England succeeded in holding on to this important colonial outpost. Note the two buglers sitting on the ground—their bugle calls would guide members of the regiment during the course of a skirmish or battle.

PANORAMIC VIEW FROM WESTMOUNT, 1899

This fascinating scene is dominated by the presence of a steam-driven British battleship at anchor, after topping up its coal bunkers at the International Coal pier on the Esplanade. Prominent in the background is the Cabot Hotel, on the right, with the Sydney Hotel and Sacred Heart Church on the left. At centre left is the majestic spire of St. George's Church on Charlotte Street.

OFFICERS BANQUET, VICTORIA PARK

Under the watchful glare of their Commander-in-Chief, King Edward VII, on the rear wall, commissioned officers (seated) and non-commissioned officers (standing) partake of a formal banquet at the Officer's Mess in Victoria Park. King Edward VII reigned from 1901 until 1910. In 1860 he became the first member of the royal family to visit North America.

ROYAL NAVY AT VICTORIA PARK

In this undated First World War photograph, officers and young seamen from the Royal Navy visit Victoria Park as guests of the Royal Navy Canadian Volunteer Reserve (RNCVR). Sitting in the front row are twelve- to fourteen-year-old "boy seamen" from the Royal Navy vessel HMS *Ackim*. Notice the tents in the background as well as the almost one-hundred-year-old barrack building on the left.

VICTORY BOND PARADE, 1915

In this photograph taken in front of the Sydney Hotel, Canadian sailors take part in a parade to sell Victory Bonds to help finance the rapidly increasing costs of the First World War. By 1915 Sydney Harbour was starting to come into its own as a staging ground for convoys heading overseas. These young men enjoy their last shore leave before heading off to escort convoys from Sydney to the British Isles.

36TH FIELD BATTERY, PARADE, 1915

The proud officers and men of the 36th Field Battery march up George Street on their way to Victoria Park, before embarking by train for further training in central Canada. Young boys, and several older men, march with them. Caught up in the patriotic fervor of the time, none of them realized that one-tenth of the group would be killed in action, while another one-fifth would be wounded.

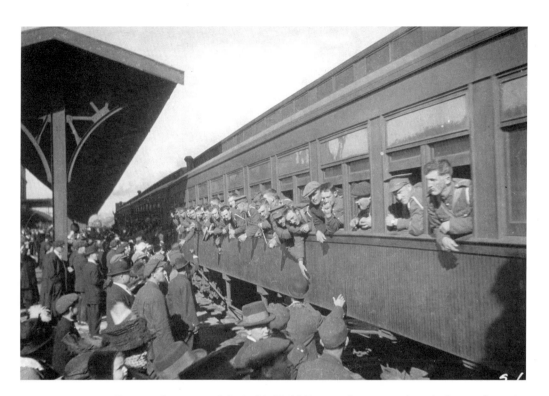

TROOP TRAIN 36TH FIELD BATTERY, 1915 Eager volunteers of the 36th Field Battery hang out the windows of a train as it prepares to leave the Intercolonial Railway station in Sydney in the fall of 1915. This local artillery unit, under the command of Major Walter Crowe, had just completed basic training at Victoria Park. After further training in central Canada, the battery was shipped overseas, arriving in France in June 1916. Over the next two years, the 36th Field Battery took part in every major campaign fought by the Canadian Army in western Europe. After hostilities ceased on November 11, 1918, the battery returned to Canada, where it was demobilized in March 1919. During the Second World War, the 36th Field Battery was reconstituted as the 36th Coast Battery, and manned several of the coastal fortifications around Sydney Harbour.

MINE SWEEPERS, C.1918

Three small naval boats with numbers on their bows are tied up next to two larger vessels at a wharf on the Esplanade, during the dying days of the First World War. This particular wharf, which later became know as the Robin Hood Wharf, is located almost directly across from the new office tower on the corner of Dorchester Street and the Esplanade. Mine Sweepers equipped with special underwater cables used to remove ("sweep") enemy mines or render them useless patrolled the waters around Sydney Harbour.

VICTORIA PARK,
OLD BARRACKS,
C.1919

This endearing photograph is of great historical significance, especially with regard to the role of Sydney as a garrison town in the early years of the British Empire. The woman and young child in the foreground also suggest the family aspect of garrison life, something which has been virtually overlooked in the military histories of Sydney.

Sydney was founded as a garrison town, and has maintained a military presence of one form or another for more than two hundred years. As such, the British soldiers who came ashore in 1785 with Governor DesBarres immediately set about to build a military installation at the tip of the peninsula on which the town would be located. Sydney remained a garrison town for the next sixty-nine years. In 1854, the last regiment was removed and sent overseas to take part in the infamous Crimean War. Before too long they were replaced by a local militia. The camp was renamed Victoria Park in 1897, in recognition of Queen Victoria's Diamond Jubilee.

The first wooden buildings included a barracks, mess hall, a small infirmary, and crude huts for the ordinary soldiers. The camp became known as Barrack Park. The three buildings seen here were built in 1833 (notice the foundations of rough field stone), and were still in use at the beginning of the Second World War, more than a hundred years later.

As an active military garrison, a handful of women would have lived in Victoria Park, from even the earliest years. Officers' wives, some with children, were known respectfully as "regiment women." Those who were not married were often referred to derogatorily as "camp followers." Whatever their status, all women in a military camp had the same chores: They cleaned, prepared food, washed clothing, and even served as nurses if the need arose. In spite of their social status, they brought a much needed sense of decorum and decency to an otherwise all-male environment.

The two men who supervised the original construction of the military park, John Muggah and Samuel Peters, both received grants of land as partial payment for their endeavors. One gave his name to Muggah Creek, which later became part of the Sydney Steel Plant, while the other received a land grant in Westmount; it later became the famous Petersfield estate.

CAPE BRETON HIGHLANDERS, 1934

Mostly kilted members of the 185th Battalion of the Cape Breton Highlanders pose at Victoria Park before taking a ship to Charlottetown, Prince Edward Island, where they will take part in military exercises. The Cape Breton Highlanders were formed in 1871 in Baddeck. Most of the founding members were Scots who could trace their ancestry back to the Highlands of Scotland. In August 1914, they were called to active duty in the First World War and were shipped overseas. In the next four years their members would earn more than 250 individual awards for bravery. In the Second World War, the Highlanders served in Italy, France, and the Netherlands. Today the Cape Breton Highlanders is a Highland militia battalion of the Canadian Armed Forces, based in the industrial area around Sydney Harbour.

HMCS
PROTECTOR

When war broke out in 1939, among the various vessels taken up for service by the Royal Canadian Navy was a motor craft that the RCMP named Protector. It was employed on various duties at Sydney, Nova Scotia. On August 28, 1939, a small establishment was set up there, and on July 22, 1940, the headquarters building was commissioned as HMCS Protector, taking its name from the motor boat, for the regulations of the time required that the name of a naval establishment be borne by some vessel afloat. Sydney became the assembly port for the slow Atlantic convoys of the SC (Sydney-Clyde) series, and a base for the ships that escorted them. It was HMCS Protector that put together the convoys, arranged their escorts, issued the sailing orders and did one-thousand-and-one other things that were necessary for the naval war effort in Cape Breton Island and surrounding waters.

A striking close-up image, taken from an altitude of three hundred feet, looking towards South Bar. These ships were part of a larger convoy that sailed from Sydney on November 7, 1940. Convoys that sailed in the late fall, or during the winter months, would often fall prey to treacherous storms and icing conditions, as well as the ever-present danger of enemy submarines.

TWENTY-THREE
SHIPS IN THE
SOUTH ARM,
1940

This image was taken from above Westmount, looking towards South Bar. Crawley's Creek flows into Sydney Harbour in the lower centre of the photograph. In the lower right is the site of the former Petersfield Estate, while the Canadian Coast Guard College is now located on the left side of the creek. Three years later, in 1943, the Point Edward Naval Base would be built in the upper left.

**122 SHIPS
AWAIT CONVOY,
1941**

Another stunning wartime image, taken from approximately five hundred feet above the entrance to Sydney Harbour, looking in. A grand total of 122 cargo ships, troop ships, and oil and gas tankers, wait in the inner harbour before joining a convoy to England. South Bar is on the left, and the Northside of Sydney Harbour is on the right.

**VICTORY TORCH,
1941**

With the Second World War well under way, an impressive "victory torch" arrived at the Sydney airport, at the beginning of a cross-Canada Victory Bonds tour. The torch was met by various high-ranking dignitaries of the Army, Navy, and Air Force, before it was transferred to Victoria Park for a massive Victory Bond parade. From Sydney, the torch made its way by train across the country to British Columbia.

"SC" also stood for "Sydney, Nova Scotia, to the river Clyde (Glasgow) in Scotland." In this remarkable photograph taken by a Royal Canadian Air Force flying boat stationed at Kelly's Beach in North Sydney, thirty-seven (out of forty-three) fully-laden merchant ships head for the west coast of Newfoundland on their way to the British Isles.

Because the normal route along the south coast of Newfoundland was so dangerous, it was decided to send this convoy through the Strait of Belle Isle, between northern Newfoundland and Labrador. It would then travel past Greenland and Iceland, and around the northern tip of Ireland. However, a combination of heavy fog and bad ice conditions resulted in serious damage to six ships, due to collisions with icebergs. All six were able to return to Sydney. At left is northern Cape Breton and Cape North.

Chapter 5

Public Service

ASHBY SCHOOL, C.1902

Ashby is that area of Sydney that stretches from the present-day Sydney Academy to Victoria Road and the overpass at the former steel plant.

Although there is no information available with regard to this photograph other than the date, it is a good example of elementary school fashion at the turn of the twentieth century. With the construction of the new steel plant well under way, the Ashby area was rapidly filling up with the children of imported workers from Newfoundland, Eastern Europe, and parts of the British Commonwealth.

TEACHER AND PUPILS, CHARLOTTE STREET, C.1862

In one of the earliest photographs taken in Sydney, teacher John Hill (top hat) and his students stand in front of their private school. As the local sheriff, Mr. Hill was responsible for keeping order not only in the classroom, but also in the community.

HOLY ANGELS CONVENT/ SCHOOL

In 1885, at the request of Sacred Heart Parish, a party of three nuns arrived in Sydney from Montreal. Members of the congregation of Notre-Dame, they had been asked to set up a school for Catholic girls. Their new wooden convent/school was waiting for them, just down the street from Sacred Heart Church. On January 4, 1886, classes began with a total of 106 students. Room and board at the facility cost $7 per month, or its equivalent in "goods or services." A northern addition of cut stone was built in 1907, and in 1953 a modern brick school was completed at the rear of the convent. Today, Holy Angels remains as the only public school for girls in Nova Scotia.

HOLY ANGELS,
CLASS OF 1908

The thirty graduates of the Class of 1908 pose in front of the brand new "northern" wing at Holy Angels convent. Made of cut stone from the local area, the new addition was completed the previous year. At that time Holy Angels had three different educational "streams," roughly comparable to elementary, junior, and senior high.

SYDNEY ACADEMY, 1902 A splendid new building of cut-stone and brick completed in February 1902. In addition to traditional classrooms, it contained a large assembly hall, library, music room, science lab, gymnasium, and a room set aside for manual training (wood-working shop).

SYDNEY
ACADEMY,
GRADUATION,
1919

The graduates of the Class of 1919 face the brighter prospect of a world at peace, only eight months after the end of the First World War in November 1918. At least the young men in this picture did not have to consider serving their king and country in the killing fields of Western Europe.

CENTRAL
SCHOOL, 1910

A combined class made up of pupils in grades five and six.

SACRED HEART CATHOLIC CHURCH, INTERIOR, c.1890

Under the direction of Father James Quinan, the first Sacred Heart Catholic Church was dedicated on December 20, 1874. Built in the Roman "Doric" style, it had three spires, with the tallest being 110 feet. In addition to Sydney, the new Sacred Heart parish included Low Point, Lingan, Point Edward, and Westmount. Only thirteen years later, on January 16, 1887, the church was completely destroyed by fire. The present church was dedicated two years later, on July 28, 1889. Approximately 100 by 50 feet, it has two spires—the one at the north corner is 135 feet, while the smaller one is 85 feet.

WOMEN'S MISSIONARY SOCIETY CONVENTION, SYDNEY, 1910

Dressed in their finest outfits, this ornate group of parishioners from various Baptist denominations in Nova Scotia gather in front of a local church for a formal portrait.

The first Canadian women's missionary society was organized at Canso, Nova Scotia, in 1870. It was set up by Maria Hannah Norris, a Baptist missionary who was born in that small fishing community. Women's Missionary Societies, which had their heyday between 1870 and 1925, were set up to preach the gospel, and to spread the word of God both overseas and in local areas.

At a time when most women were confined to the home, these societies provided an opportunity to meet in church-sponsored activities that included bake sales, teas, quilting sessions, and other fund-raising activities. That money was used to buy clothing and medical supplies that could be sent to foreign missions. In larger urban areas, money was often donated to help defray the construction costs of schools and hospitals.

ST. NICHOLAS   During the first decade of the twentieth century, a substantial Italian
ITALIAN CHURCH   immigrant community had developed in Whitney Pier and Ashby. Drawn
(ROMAN   to the area by the construction of the steel plant and the development
CATHOLIC),   of nearby coal mines, their religious needs were served by a non-Italian,
WHITNEY PIER   English-speaking pastor in a nearby parish. All that changed in 1911 when
Father Domenico Viola arrived from Italy. He immediately set about to
build a new church, specifically for the needs of the Italian community, on
the corner of William and Hankard streets in Whitney Pier.

Completed in 1912, the new wooden church of St. Nicholas in the
North End was of Gothic design, with an imposing sixty-five-foot
tower and steeple. For the first number of years the building, which
could seat 350 people, also served as a glebe house for Father Viola and
Father Ronald MacLean who succeeded him. Although the mass was
in traditional Latin, there were two sermons: one in Italian and one in
English.

The parish of St. Nicholas also served a large number of non-Italian
families in Whitney Pier and Ashby. This included a sizeable number of
Newfoundlanders, as well as a significant number of families from the
West Indies. St. Nicholas Church was destroyed by fire in 1975, and
replaced by a cultural centre on Gatacre Street, where mass is held each
Sunday. The parish now consists of about fifty families, and religious
services are provided by clergy from Holy Redeemer Parish.

Back in 1919 the visit of the spiritual head of the Roman Catholic Church in eastern Nova Scotia to one of his outlying parishes was almost equivalent to a papal visit in today's terms. For months beforehand the parish would be preoccupied with plans for the visit, and everything would be planned in detail. The pomp and spectacle of the Catholic religion would be put on full display.

Such was the scene on October 26, 1919, when Bishop James Morrison of the Diocese of Antigonish arrived in Whitney Pier. He, along with a substantial entourage, was on hand to officially consecrate the new Holy Redeemer Church. In this photograph, taken on the steps of the local convent, the bishop and four of his clergy are surrounded by an honour guard formed by the Knights of Columbus, a Catholic men's organization. In the background, on the verandah, local altar boys maintain a respectful demeanor during the celebrations.

The Diocese of Antigonish includes the counties of Antigonish, Pictou, and Guysborough, and all of Cape Breton Island. When originally formed in Arichat, in 1844, it was known as the Diocese of Arichat. In 1858 the seat was moved to Antigonish, on the mainland.

HOLY REDEEMER, NAVE — Altar boys, Knights of Columbus Honour Guard (with sashes), and parishioners gather in the nave of the uncompleted church, while a hundred more remain outside the main door, waiting for their chance to enter for the ceremonies with the bishop.

VICTORIA METHODIST CHURCH, 1924

In 1901 a large wooden building was constructed on Victoria Road in Whitney Pier. With a high gable roof and two levels of windows, it was copied from early New England building styles. This structure was to serve as a mission church of the Sydney Jubilee Methodist Church. In 1925 the Mission Church was renamed the Victoria United Church, although it continued to be known as Victoria Methodist church. The congregation included many Newfoundlanders and West Indians, and other Anglo-Celtic immigrants and migrants from various parts of Nova Scotia, including Black Nova Scotians.

The Victoria Methodist Church, one of the major components of the United Church in Whitney Pier, is no longer active. Nor is the building standing, having been demolished soon after the Methodist congregation joined Trinity Church in 1937. It is now the site of the Royal Canadian Legion.

The insert photo is of the Rev. James G. Staney, minister from 1904–1914.

**St. Andrew's
United Church**

In 1852 a small Scottish Presbyterian church by the name of St. Andrew's was built on north Charlotte Street, under the direction of the Rev. Hugh MacLeod. By 1888 a second building was erected on Pitt Street, in order to handle a rapidly growing congregation. Then, in 1909, a newly arrived minister by the name of Rev. John Pringle decided to build a more impressive structure on Bentinck Street, virtually next door to the old building. This photograph shows the new edifice in 1914, only two years after it opened. On the right, in the background, is the "second" St. Andrew's. In 1925 the Methodist church, the Congregationalist church, and sixty per cent of the Presbyterian churches in Canada joined together to form the United Church of Canada. St. Andrew's became part of the new denomination.

DIAMOND JUBILEE BIBLE CLASS, 1911

Looking rather stern and proper, this bible class from St. Andrew's Church poses for the camera on the church steps, October 2, 1911. Rev. John Pringle, the new minister of the parish, is in the top right-hand corner.

St. George's Church

This festive image from 1926 was taken on Charlotte Street, during Old Home Week ceremonies. The Homecoming Queen, riding in her convertible, has a naval escort with rifles and bayonets marching in front. The photograph also shows two of the many fine historical properties to be found in the north end of the city—St. Georges Church and the James Clarke house.

St. George's Church was built between 1785 and 1790 for Rev. Ranna Cossitt, and is the oldest church in Sydney. It was erected by British engineers from the 33rd Regiment stationed at Victoria Park, and became known as the "Garrison Church." Most of the structure was built of stone taken from the ruined walls of Fortress Louisbourg. It was granted a royal charter by King George III, thus making it the official place of worship for the royal family, should they ever visit Cape Breton. (They never did.)

To the left of the church is a Queen Anne style home, built in 1896 by James Clarke, owner of the Sydney Foundry & Engineering Works (later Sydney Engineering & Drydock). It displays many classical influences such as arches, and round and Palladian windows. Its most distinguishing feature, however, is the unconventional tower attached to the southwest corner of the house.

St. George's Ukrainian Parishioners, c.1940

This rather formal photo of the Ukrainian congregation was taken during the early years of the World War Two. The Ukrainian community was only one of many ethnic groups from central and eastern Europe to come to Sydney in search of employment in the new steel plant.

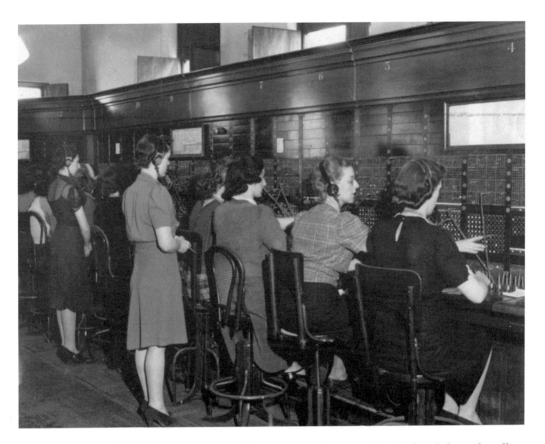

MARITIME TELEGRAPH & TELEPHONE COMPANY OPERATORS, SYDNEY, 1940

Telephone operators, with two supervisors standing behind them, handle incoming and outgoing calls using manual switchboards in the winter of 1940. With the start of the Second World War in 1939, the volume of military-related calls increased dramatically, especially with regard to Victoria Park and the various coastal defence installations around Sydney Harbour.

Commercial telephone service in Cape Breton started back in 1890, with the establishment of the Eastern Telephone Company in Sydney. This business bought out several small local exchanges in the industrial area around Sydney. By 1901 telephone service to Halifax and other mainland points became available with the completion of an underwater cable across the Strait of Canso. By 1905 there were 923 telephones in the industrial area.

Two operators in the foreground handle all "directory-assistance" calls at the Sydney office, while in the background a total of twenty switchboard operators handle routine traffic in or out of the Sydney exchange. The large vertical file in the centre of the photograph contained an alphabetical listing of all telephone numbers in the Sydney area.

Chapter 6

Sports, Leisure, and Entertainment

ALEX GILLIS AND THE INVERNESS SERENADERS, 1923

A treasured family photograph portrays in the front row, from left to right: Bernie Gillis (S.W. Margaree), Mike MacLean (Iona), Jack Gillis (S.W. Margaree), Alex Gillis (S.W. Margaree); back row: Peter MacIntyre (Benacadie), Joe Walker (Lake Ainslie), Alex MacIntyre (Benacadie).

The Gillises from South West Margaree, were all accomplished fiddlers and carpenters who played and worked in the Sydney area in the early 1920s. Bernie, Jack and Alex later moved to "The Boston States," and were featured performers on a weekly radio show from Boston called "Alex Gillis and the Inverness Serenaders." They were descendants of Malcolm Gillis (The Margaree Bard), who was an accomplished fiddler, poet, and composer of Gaelic songs. He also found time to father eighteen children. (The bottle of whisky on top of the very elaborate fiddle case was undoubtedly there for medicinal purposes.)

BLACK AND WHITE HOCKEY TEAM, 1900

Looking like a bunch of convicts with their striped shirts, this team from Sydney won the Cape Breton Hockey Championship for the 1899–1900 season. Front row: W. Buchanan, W. Tobin, W. Langille; middle row: H. Moffatt; H. MacNeil, W. Cann, J. Collins; top row: J. Robertson (president), A. Purves (referee).

DOMINION IRON AND STEEL COMPANY HOCKEY TEAM, 1901

While their hockey equipment may have been rather primitive, especially the skates and shin pads, the trophy for the Cape Breton Hockey League, which went to this team from the steel company, was elaborate. This photograph is particularly interesting because it listed the position that each man played. Front row: F. Ball (goalie), F. Lucas (cover point), B. Purves (centre); F. Slade (right wing), M. Eagan (left wing); back row: A. Cruise (president), J. Gould (manager), C. Hearn (rover), E. Cummings (point), J. Whitman (substitute)

SYDNEY MILLIONAIRES, 1913, STANLEY CUP FINALISTS

This 1913 photograph of the players and management of the Sydney Millionaires was taken after they won the title "Champions of the Maritime Professional Hockey Association." They immediately boarded a train for Montreal, where they lost the Stanley Cup to the Quebec Bulldogs. They were one of only two Maritime teams to compete for the Stanley Cup in the years before the trophy was taken over by the National Hockey League in the 1920s.

SYDNEY MILLIONAIRES, 1939

The Millionaires were considered one of the best teams in eastern Canada, and in the next ten years, from winning the provincial championship in 1939, they only got better. In 1941 they defeated two Quebec teams, from Hull and Montreal, and then traveled by train across the country to Regina, where they lost to the Regina Rangers for the Allan Cup. In 1949 they advanced to the eastern Canadian finals, for the Allan Cup, against the mighty Toronto Marlboros. The games were played in Maple Leaf Gardens, where the powerful Marlboros finally won, in overtime of the final game! By the early 1950s the Cape Breton Senior Hockey League was considered one of the best leagues in Canada, with teams in Sydney, North Sydney, and Glace Bay.

SYDNEY CAPITALS BASEBALL TEAM, C.1910

Although baseball played second fiddle to hockey, it was nevertheless a very popular seasonal sport in Cape Breton. Teams could be found in Sydney, Glace Bay, New Waterford, and on the Northside. By the 1930s the Cape Breton Colliery Baseball League was a powerful four-team circuit made up of American imports and local players. The teams played to sellout crowds, and many of the players would go on to "minor" careers in the professional leagues.

Sydney
Academy
Rugby Team,
1923

Rugby was introduced to Sydney in the early years of the nineteenth century by the British troops stationed at Victoria Park. When the garrison was removed in the 1850s, the game ceased to be played locally. However, by the turn of the twentieth century, there was a large influx of workers from the British Isles to the industrial towns of Cape Breton, as a result of the rapid development of the coal and steel industry. The sport was revived, and continued to be played in local communities up until the Second World War. It is seldom played today, having been replaced by Canadian football, or, more recently, soccer.

THE ESPLANADE,   This photograph looking south along the Esplanade was taken circa 1901.
C.1901   The newly constructed building on the right is the Cape Breton Yacht
Club. The club received its Royal Warrant the following year. At this time
the horse and wagon was still the primary means of transportation in the
Sydney area, and the roads were still nothing more than dirt or gravel cart
tracks. In periods of heavy rain, or during the spring thaw, many of them
became virtually impassable.

ROYAL CAPE BRETON YACHT CLUB, 1905

From as far back as 1850, Sydney merchant John Bourinot, the first French consul in British North America, had held organized sailboat races in front of his elegant home on the waterfront. His imposing residence at what later came to be known as Robin Hood Wharf quickly became the social centre of the town, and served as Sydney's unofficial yacht club until a disastrous fire in 1899. Later that year a select group of individuals gathered at the Sydney Hotel. Present were high-ranking officials of the Dominion Coal Company and the new Dominion Iron & Steel Company, along with prominent members of the Sydney community. When the evening was over, the Cape Breton Yacht Club had been formed, the club's officers elected, and the club charter and by-laws approved. A.J. Moxham, the general manager of the Dominion Iron & Steel Company, was elected the first commodore. The first order of business was to purchase a building site on the waterfront.

Sir William Cornelius Van Horne, president of the Canadian Pacific Railway, and his son made sketches of the clubhouse, which they designed to resemble the former Bourinot residence just up the street. Richard Sturgiss, a well-known architect from Boston, was commissioned to draw up the plans. The official opening took place on December 18, 1900.

The founding members of the new yacht club had impeccable connections, both in Ottawa and with the British government, including royalty. In December 1900, the club applied for an Admiralty Warrant, which would allow vessels registered to the club to fly the Blue Ensign of His Majesty's Fleet. This was a very special distinction available to only a few yacht clubs in the British Commonwealth. In January 1901, the application was granted. The club immediately applied for a Royal Warrant, which would allow it to add the word "Royal" to its name. This was a very special distinction, and one that was seldom granted. This application took a little longer, but by April 1902, the club had received notification of King Edward II's approval, and in April 1903, after a special act was passed by the Legislative Assembly of the province of Nova Scotia, the club was incorporated as The Royal Cape Breton Yacht Club.

SYDNEY CORNET BAND, 1901

This photograph of the Sydney Cornet Band, with other returning veterans, was taken on its return from the Boer War in the winter of 1901. This musical ensemble came into existence in 1884, when they took over the instruments of the "Sydney Band," the first brass band formed in Sydney, in 1870. The bandmaster of the new group was Tomas Gillespie, a Sydney native who was born in the old military barracks in Victoria Park. He joined the famed Black Watch, and served with the regiment in India for a period of twelve years. Upon his return, he formed this band, which lasted for more than twenty years. The band raised its own funds to build an elaborate bandstand on the Esplanade, across from the new Masonic Hall.

BRASS BAND, LAURIER STREET, 1921

This evocative photograph, taken in Whitney Pier, shows band members of "The United Negro Improvement Association" (1918–1932), one of several brass bands based in different parts of the city. The approximately twenty members of the band were under the direction of Bandmaster Colin MacDonald. The parade, along streets with no sidewalks or pavement, was in support of an international protest movement proposing "Africa for the Africans!"

THE GREAT MOUSTACHE CONTEST, C.1903

Mustachioed officers (bottom centre) from a visiting French warship mingle with local guests and British officers from Victoria Park, at a social event held at the Royal Cape Breton Yacht Club during Regatta Week. The gentleman with the finest moustache would receive an award.

THE SEVEN LAST WORDS OF CHRIST.
LYCEUM THEATRE.
APL 9TH 1909.

HAYDN'S ORATORIO, LYCEUM THEATRE, 1909

The oratorio *The Seven Last Words of Christ* by Franz Joseph Haydn was performed at the Lyceum Theatre on April 9, 1909. In this formal photograph, the singers and members of the orchestra pose in front of the mighty pipe organ, an instrument that was a special feature of religious programs held at the venue. An oratorio is a musical drama, performed without actions, costumes, or scenery. Usually based on Biblical or historical themes, they involve soloists, a chorus, and a small orchestra.

The lyceum was originally conceived as an opera house, and was built by the Roman Catholic Diocese of Antigonish in 1904. The design included a gymnasium, library, billiards room, and clubrooms, as well as a lovely theatre seating nine hundred people!

A major fire in 1951 gutted the interior, but it was quickly remodeled and re-opened in 1952 as Xavier Junior College, the Sydney campus of St. Francis Xavier University in Antigonish. Today it is the home of the Old Sydney Society.

SYDNEY RIFLE CLUB, C.1910

This well-armed group of hunters, all members of the Sydney Rifle Club, pose for an interesting photograph before setting out, in much smaller groups, to their assigned hunting locations in several rural areas outside the city. Only four years later, with the outbreak of the First World War, some of the younger members of this party would be on their way overseas as members of the Canadian Expeditionary Force. There they would face the distinctly unpleasant possibility of being shot in No Man's Land, far from the peace and tranquility of their native island.

STAFF OF CJCB
RADIO, 1935

CJCB, Cape Breton's first radio station, went on the air on February 14, 1928. The producer was Nathaniel (Nate) Nathanson, who owned the music and book store from which the broadcasts originated. Nate had not been able to sell very many radios, the newest technological marvel, because there was very little to listen to. After dark, and if the atmospheric conditions were right, two or three American stations could sometimes be picked up, but these were sporadic at the best of times. To increase sales, Nate bought a used ship's radio, and altered it to work on land. For the first year, his new station was on the air for two hours at lunch time and three hours in the evening. In 1935 the staff of CJCB radio included (left to right): Charlie Atkinson; Robby Robertson; Charlie MacDougall; Gordon O'Brien; Fred Kyte; Hal Stephens; and Hugh Gorman.

Some CJCB highlights from the last seventy-five years:

February 1930. A night clerk at a Sydney hotel was murdered. CJCB was asked to broadcast a description of the subject, who was recognized and later arrested in Point Edward.

August 1934. A new and more powerful radio transmitter went on the air from a hill in South Bar.

September 1936. Beryl Markham, the first woman to fly the Atlantic Ocean from east to west, made a crash landing in a bog at Baleine, just up the coast from Louisbourg. CJCB was soon on the scene and the "remote" report was carried around the world.

December 1938. A thick rope used to haul cars of miners out of the pit at Princess Colliery in Sydney Mines broke, and the cars hurtled down a sloping shaft to crash together at the bottom. Twenty-one men were killed, and dozens more injured. CJCB reported from the pithead, and an appeal for funds resulted in the grand total of $14,000 being raised for the families of the dead miners. That was a small fortune in the Great Depression.

September 1948. The Canadian Broadcasting Company (CBC) opened its own radio station in Sydney. Sydney now had two stations, Cape Breton Island (CBI) and CJCB.

April 1962. CJCB launched Cape Breton's first FM station: CKPE-FM.

COTTAR'S SATURDAY NIGHT (CJCB), 1935

Members of the cast of "Cottar's Saturday Night" dress up in appropriate costume to reflect the Scottish nature of this popular local radio program. Originating at station CJCB in Sydney, this musical and variety show was carried live across Canada on the national network.

Back row: Mrs. J.R. MacKimmie, Malcolm MacLeod, Bernie MacIntosh, Mose Ballah, Mrs. Bleddyn Davies, Mrs. William Matheson.

Seated: John MacNeil, Mrs. C.D. Buck, Bleddyn Davies, Tena Campbell, Mabel Kelliher, Bob Wright, G.W. MacDonald, Sandy MacLean

Chapter 7

Homes and Family

THE PETERSFIELD ESTATE, WESTMOUNT

The origin of this estate dates back to shortly after the founding of Sydney. In 1787 Colonel Samuel Peters, a United Empire Loyalist, was granted this piece of land by the British Government. The land remained undeveloped, and eventually became know as "Petersfield."

In the latter part of the nineteenth century the property was bought by John Stewart (J.S.) McLennan, a Montreal-born businessman who had completed his education at Cambridge University in England. He moved to Cape Breton because he was intrigued by the construction of the largest and most modern steel plant in Canada in this rather remote provincial location.

In 1904 he bought the local newspaper, the *Sydney Post*, and renamed it the *Sydney Post Record*. He became interested in the Fortress ruins at Louisbourg, and in 1918 wrote a best selling book—*Louisbourg: From its Foundation to its Fall*—which is still in print eighty-five years later.

In July 1901, McLellan and his family moved into their new home, "Petersfield," in Point Edward. The estate overlooking the harbour contained several buildings including a studio, boathouse, stables, caretaker's cottage, tennis courts, and several gardens. The two-storey family house was built in the style of an Italian villa, with seventeen rooms and an elevator.

Needless to say, Petersfield quickly became the social centre of the Sydney area, and invitations to the many functions that were held there were highly sought after. In the years before World War One, distinguished individuals who visited and often stayed there included: Canadian Governor General Lord Grey (of Grey Cup fame), Sir Wilfred Grenfell, Lord Louis Mountbatten (great-grandson of Queen Victoria and uncle to the duke of Edinburgh), and many captains and officers from British, French, and American warships visiting Sydney Harbour.

Between the two world wars, the Petersfield guest book continued to list the names of world-class visitors: Canadian prime ministers Arthur Meighen and R.B. Bennett, British prime minister Ramsay MacDonald, Governors-General Byng, Willingdon, and Tweedsmuir; Lord and Lady Baden-Powell, Alexander Graham Bell, Casey Baldwin, and many others.

J.S. McLennan died in 1939. In the summer of 1941 the estate was expropriated by the Canadian military for use as an officer's residence. After the war the estate fell into disrepair. The exhilarating days of pomp and circumstance at Petersfield are long gone. The former estate is now a provincial park and all that remains of its glory days are several stone foundations.

COLBY, 1840   This is undoubtedly the earliest known photograph taken in Sydney. In 1817, Captain William Cox, a British Army officer stationed at Victoria Park, applied for a grant of land near the bottom of Hardwood Hill. When the grant was approved, he named the new house that he built on the property "Colby," after the name of his family estate in England.

BURCHELL FAMILY, C.1861   An excellent example of women's fashions in the middle of the nineteenth century. Taken in front of their home on Charlotte Street (next to Cossit House), this group photo is perhaps the earliest taken in Sydney. The Burchell family, from Ireland, included highly respected local businessmen involved in coal mines, law, and real estate.

JUDGES CORNER, C.1870   The unpretentious home of two judges, A.C. and E.M. Dodd, on the corner of Esplanade and Dorchester streets overlooking the harbour. Known at the time as "Judges Corner," it would later be the location of the Sydney Hotel, the Isle Royale Hotel, and the present-day Commerce Tower (Canadian Imperial Bank of Commerce).

THE NORTH END, C.1897   This interesting shot of the North End, taken from the Esplanade in the late 1890s, shows the twin balconies of the Bourinot House in the near foreground. In the background, on the skyline, is visible the steeple of St. George's Church, the cupola or small dome-like structure on the roof of Holy Angels Convent, and the cupola on top of the old courthouse in Victoria Park. The small buildings on the shore mark the present location of the Sydney Marine Terminal, home to many visiting cruise ships.

BOURINOT HOUSE, C.1895

Four very important buildings from the turn of the twentieth century are pictured in this photograph from the harbour looking south.

The Bourinot House (c.1788–90) on the shore in the left of the photo was built shortly after the founding of Sydney in 1785. Immediately behind it is the Sydney Hotel, built in 1896. The small wooden building, on the (present-day) corner of Dorchester Street and the Esplanade, was the Masonic Hall. The large building on the water side of the Esplanade was the Cabot Hotel.

The Bourinot House was constructed by the Honorable John George Bourinot, a successful merchant and one of the most remarkable men who ever lived in Sydney. In his long and very active life, he served as a Conservative member of the Nova Scotia House of Assembly, the local agent for Lloyd's Insurance of London, England, a well-respected notary public, and colonel in charge of the Sydney Militia. In 1850 he was also appointed the first French consul in British North America. He was the father of Sir John Bourinot, the well-known historian, who was born in Sydney in 1837.

The large, white, three-story building had a long, two-level veranda, on the three sides facing the harbour. Without a doubt the most impressive structure on the Sydney waterfront from the 1850s onward, the Bourinot House was often used to entertain the officers of visiting French and British warships stopped in Sydney to obtain coal. It was also the scene of many prestigious social events, and in the 1880s and 1890s was the meeting place for the Sydney Yacht Club. It was badly damaged by a fire in 1899, after which it was used as a temporary warehouse. It was finally torn down in 1903.

VIEW OF BOURINOT HOUSE AND SYDNEY HOTEL, C.1897

WILLOW TOP COTTAGE, 1897   This small, old-fashioned house with a vine-covered porch in front occupied a prominent location on Dorchester Street. In the 1870s and 80s it served as a hotel. Perhaps its most distinguished visitor arrived on August 19, 1880. The Marquis of Lorne, governor general of Canada, brought his own personal bagpiper with him, and was serenaded during his meals by the musician, who paraded back and forth outside the building, much to the amusement of the neighbours and passers-by.

BROOKLAND STREET, C.1900 This view of a quiet residential street, from the corner of Brookland and High streets, looks west towards George Street. On this postcard scene, the name of the street is misspelled in the top left corner.

MOSELEY HOUSE, 1900 This dwelling, owned by one of Sydney's better known businessmen, stood on King's Road, overlooking Wentworth Park, where the former Nazareth House, a maternity home run by the Catholic Church, was located.

MOXHAM'S CASTLE, 1902

Arthur James Moxham was born in Glamorganshire, South Wales, in 1854. His father, an architect, died while he was a young child, and he was placed in the Clapham Orphan Asylum near London. In spite of its name, the asylum was actually a boarding school, from which A.J. graduated in 1869, at the age of fifteen. With the blessing of his mother, the young lad set out by boat for the United States, determined to make his fortune.

He settled in Louisville, Kentucky, and went to work in the Louisville Rolling Mills, a foundry and iron mill. He was fascinated with the process of making iron, and soon was taking evening courses that would eventually lead to an engineering diploma. In 1878, A.J. moved his young family to Birmingham, Alabama, where he designed and supervised the construction of the Birmingham Rolling Mills Company. He was only twenty-four years old.

In the early 1880s he joined with two other individuals to form the Johnson Steel Rail Company, to produce steel rails for streetcars or railways. Within a few years, the business had expanded to such an extent that the company was making ninety per cent of all the steel rails produced in the United States. Although the vast expansion of the railroad system in the United States was primarily responsible for the company's great success, A.J. Moxham's ingenuity with regard to organization and supervision of production procedures had an equally important role to play. In 1894 the company moved to Lorain, Ohio, where they built a much larger rail mill and new and improved blast furnaces.

In anticipation of this move, Moxham had supervised the construction of a replica of a Scottish clan castle in thick woods just outside the city of Lorain. It had four floors, thirty rooms including thirteen bedrooms, an auditorium on the fourth floor, and a swimming pool in the basement! His wife, Helen, and five children were said to have been delighted. By 1896 Moxham had decided to cash in his shares in the steel company. He retired a very wealthy man, at the young age of forty-two.

It seems that he had a life-long ambition to sail around the world in his own yacht. With this in mind, he went to England, bought a 560-ton steam-powered yacht, and set sail across the Atlantic Ocean. When he stopped in Boston, he made the acquaintance of a local businessman by the name of H.M. Whitney, who was promoting the construction of a new steel plant in Sydney, Nova Scotia. The state-of-the-art plant would be called the Dominion Iron and Steel Company.

Mr. Whitney made Moxham an offer he could not refuse, so he cancelled his world cruise and formed a partnership with the Boston financier. He sailed for Sydney, where he supervised the construction of the new steel plant. His wife, however, was not pleased; she was reportedly against moving to this unknown city on the edge of North America, not wanting to give up her new castle in Ohio. Being a realist and a man of action, A. J. Moxham decided to dismantle his castle, ship it to Nova Scotia, and have it rebuilt on the edge of Sydney Harbour. Reluctantly, Mrs. Moxham agreed.

Both of their sons, Tom and Egbert, apprenticed at the new steel plant. Tragically, the eldest son, Tom, a plant foreman and only twenty-five years of age, was killed on June 5, 1901, while supervising the loading of rail cars at the mill. Tom's wife, Ellen, expecting their first child, decided to remain in Sydney until after the birth. But two months later, Ellen died after her child was stillborn. All three were taken by train to Louisville for burial.

Needless to say, the three deaths in such quick succession drained the spirit from Arthur and Helen Moxham. Finally, late in 1902, Moxham decided to leave Sydney and his castle, and accept a position at a new steel plant in the United States. He never returned to Nova Scotia, and died in Long Island, New York, in 1931.

The castle remained empty from 1902 until the outbreak of the First World War in 1914. It was then taken over by the Canadian government for use as a convalescent military hospital. After the war, the castle passed through several families, the last leaving in 1960. Moxham's Castle, one of only two such structures in all of Canada, was destroyed by fire in 1966.

MOXHAM'S CASTLE, C.1902

In this charming winter scene, Arthur James Moxham stands in front of his new home overlooking Sydney Harbour. He would return to the United States before the year was over.

MOXHAM'S CASTLE, INTERIOR, C.1917

This rare photograph of the castle interior was taken during World War One, at the time when Moxham's Castle had been taken over by the Department of National Defence for use as a military hospital. All of the soldiers on the ground floor had either been wounded in action on the Western Front in France, or were survivors of the first devastating poison gas attacks that took place in 1916 and 1917.

BURCHELL HOUSE, ESPLANADE, C.1910

This rather domineering structure was built in 1901 by John E. Burchell, manager of the Royal Bank of Canada. Built to his own design and specifications, it was the first house in eastern Nova Scotia to be constructed of reinforced concrete! The concrete was mixed and poured on the spot, by local tradesmen, who had previously only built wooden homes. Nevertheless, it was considered to be a showpiece of modern construction technology, and people came from all over Nova Scotia to view it.

WHITNEY AVENUE, C.1910

An interesting photograph of an electric streetcar on Whitney Avenue. The steeple of the Baptist church is on the left. At this time most Sydney streets outside of the downtown core were not paved, resulting in very muddy conditions with the arrival of the spring thaw.

CARETAKER'S COTTAGE, PETERSFIELD

By 1914, the Petersfield estate had expanded to include a boathouse, stables, a studio, large gazebo, tennis courts, and a one-level cottage for the caretaker. As well as being responsible for all buildings on the estate, the caretaker also supervised several gardens, in particular the extensive rose garden.

Chapter 8

People

ROYAL VISIT, 1951

A young Princess Elizabeth tours the Sydney steel plant with her husband, Prince Philip, during the royal visit to the Maritime Provinces in the summer of 1951. While various dignitaries and security people hover in the background, the royal couple look over a row of ingot moulds in the blast furnace. When Elizabeth's father, King George VI, died in 1952, she became the Queen of England and the British Commonwealth.

REV. RANNA
COSSITT—
RECTOR OF
ST. GEORGE'S
CHURCH FROM
1786–1805

Cossitt House, in the historic North End, is the oldest home still standing in the city. It was built in 1787 by the Reverend Ranna Cossitt, Anglican minister in charge of the chapel at the nearby military garrison. A native of New Hampshire, and the first Protestant Minister in Cape Breton, he arrived with his wife and seven children expecting to move into the new parsonage that he had been promised. Neither it, nor the new church, had been built, although the lumber had been ordered by Lieutenant Governor Joseph DesBarres.

With typical Yankee ingenuity, Cossitt built his own house on Charlotte Street, a relatively simple salt box structure in the New England style. He then supervised the construction of nearby St. George's Church. He sold the house in 1826, and it was remodeled and enlarged around 1900. After changing hands a total of thirteen times since 1826, the building was bought by the government of Nova Scotia in 1975. Under the care of the Old Sydney Society, it has been restored with authentic eighteenth-century furniture, and costumed guides show visitors around during the summer months.

Mrs. Dorothy and Mr. Samuel Rigby, c.1850

Perhaps the earliest portrait photograph taken in Sydney. Dorothy Rigby was the daughter of Mr. and Mrs. William Cox, the first people to settle in Coxheath.

NELSON MUGGAH, 1889

This prominent Sydney businessman was a direct descendant of one of Sydney's first settlers. Back in 1785, John Muggah was one of two individuals in charge of the construction of the first military buildings at Victoria Park. As partial payment, in lieu of cash, he was granted a large section of land on the east side of a nearby creek. Muggah Creek later became part of the Sydney steel industrial complex, and today is part of the infamous Sydney Tar Ponds.

COMMODORE ROBERT PEARY AND HIS FAMILY, SYDNEY HARBOUR, SEPTEMBER 1909

Commodore Robert Peary was an accomplished civil engineer and surveyor, as well as a officer in the United States Navy. On two occasions he surveyed possible routes through the jungles of Central America before the construction of the Panama Canal. He later developed a passion for Arctic exploration.

On April 6, 1909, Commodore Peary became the first non-aboriginal person to reach the North Pole. With him were his Black assistant, Matthew Henson, and five Inuit companions.

On his return from this historic voyage, he stopped in Sydney Harbour on September 6, in order to send telegrams regarding his accomplishment to his supporters and the media. Photographer Charles Walter Kelly was given exclusive rights to photograph the Commodore and other members of the ship's crew while they were in Sydney.

Matthew Henson was born in Maryland in 1866, the son of former slaves. At the age of twelve he got a job as cabin boy on a sailing ship, and spent the rest of his life at sea. For a period of eighteen years he accompanied Peary on his explorations in the Canadian Arctic.

Commodore Peary received many awards and commendations for his conquest of the North Pole in 1909. However, it was not until 1945 that Henson finally received belated recognition from the United States government for his part in this great accomplishment. It appears that Henson was quite surprised to find that there was a sizeable Black community in Sydney. Needless to say, he was treated like a conquering hero, and never forgot his warm welcome in the "Steel City."

NORTH POLE
SLED, SYDNEY,
1909

Two crew members of Peary's ship, the S.S. *Roosevelt*, model their Arctic
garments for C.W. Kelly's lens while on their visit to Cape Breton.

GEORGE
WARDWELL,
1909

The chief engineer on the S.S. *Roosevelt* strikes an intimidating pose for
C.W. Kelly's camera.

THE *ROOSEVELT* ARRIVES IN SYDNEY   On the morning of September 6, 1909, Commodore Peary's ship, the S.S. *Roosevelt,* arrives at the ferry wharf in Sydney. In this fascinating photograph, the ship approaches the Cape Breton Electric Company dock, where hundreds of people are waiting to greet them. Also on hand were several bands, various local dignitaries, and government officials. A reception was held that evening at the Royal Cape Breton Yacht Club. Robert Peary had influential backers for his attempt to reach the North Pole. The most prominent were President Theodore Roosevelt and the National Geographic Society. With their support he was able to design and build an ice-reinforced vessel for his dash to the pole.

COAL BANK CREW, C.1910

Hugh Hill (extreme left), was the foreman of this large crew that worked for the Sydney and Louisbourg Railway. The coal bank was located just off Victoria Road, near the overpass at the former steel plant. Coal from mines in New Waterford and Glace Bay would be stockpiled at the bank, before being sent on to the steel plant, the Intercolonial Railroad Station, or to homes and fish plants in Louisbourg.

Coal Boat Captains, c.1920

These five distinguished gentlemen were captains of Dominion Coal Company Boats that delivered Cape Breton coal to various ports on the eastern seaboard of Canada or the United States. From left to right: H. Gould (SS *Louisbourg*), D. Fraser (SS *Bonavista*), R. Fraser (SS *Coban*), T. Whalen (SS *Cacauna*), J. Reid (SS *Cape Breton*).

**JAMES
McCONNELL,
C.1924**

This Sydney businessman was mayor of Sydney from 1924–1931. An avid reader and lover of books, he made a substantial monetary donation in the fall of 1959 to help replace the former Sydney Library, which was lost to fire, along with more than 80,000 books. The new library building, which opened in 1960, is know as The James McConnell Memorial Library.

Executive of the Sydney Local 1064, United Steelworkers of America, on the steps of the union hall in Whitney Pier. By the mid-1930s, in the midst of the Great Depression, an international movement arose to organize and unite all American and Canadian workers in mass-production industries. This quickly led to the rise of international unions such as the United Steelworkers and the United Autoworkers. Steelworkers in Cape Breton, under the leadership of Silby Barrett, formed a local union in 1936. When a contract was signed with the management of Sydney Steel, Local 1064 became the earliest steelworker local in Canada.

**COMMANDER
R. D. MITCHELL,
1941**

Commander Mitchell, naval control service officer, was in charge of the trans-Atlantic convoys leaving Sydney during the Second World War. He was British, and a retired commander of the Royal Navy, who happened to be living in Canada when the war broke out. He was called back to full service, seconded to the Royal Canadian Navy, and assigned to oversee convoy operations in Cape Breton.

EARL OF ATHLONE, 1943, POINT EDWARD NAVAL BASE

The Earl of Athlone stands tall on his first visit to the new naval base at Point Edward, in the summer of 1943. To his left is Captain Schwerdt, commanding officer of the naval base, while on the right is Commander Mitchell, officer in charge of all convoys leaving Sydney for overseas.

The Earl of Athlone (Prince Alexander of Teck) served as governor general of Canada from 1940 to 1946. An uncle to George VI, the king of England, he was a military man who had served with distinction in the Boer War (South Africa) and in the trenches of the First World War in Western Europe.

Prior to the construction of the naval base, the Canadian Navy made use of commercial wharves in Sydney, and requisitioned office buildings on Charlotte Street and the Esplanade. The Point Edward Naval Base closed in 1965.